ASSURANCES

ASSURANCES

J. O. Morgan

CAPE POETRY

1 3 5 7 9 10 8 6 4 2

Jonathan Cape, an imprint of Vintage,
20 Vauxhall Bridge Road,
London SW1V 2SA

Jonathan Cape is part of the Penguin Random House group of companies
whose addresses can be found at global.penguinrandomhouse.com

Penguin
Random House
UK

First published by Jonathan Cape in 2018

penguin.co.uk/vintage

A CIP catalogue record for this book is available
from the British Library

ISBN 9781787330856

Typeset in 11/13 pt Bembo by Jouve (UK), Milton Keynes
Printed and bound in Great Britain by TJ International Ltd, Padstow, Cornwall

Penguin Random House is committed to a sustainable future for
our business, our readers and our planet. This book is made
from Forest Stewardship Council® certified paper.

*. . . have I then done so grievously amiss
that by no means it may be amended?*

Thomas Wyatt

During the early years of the Cold War my father, in his capacity as an R.A.F. officer, was involved in that aspect of bomber-command which dealt with maintaining the *Airborne Nuclear Deterrent*, as it then was. The following takes what I've gleaned of his role over those years and represents it here as a work of variations and possibilities. The scenario itself may be one of routine and repetition, but what I've chosen to draw from it is the undercurrent of waiting, in the ever-present awareness of what is lost when such a waiting is permitted to play out.

J.O.

ASSURANCES

Born from a need to counteract the threat.
Now that such a threat.
For threats have been made.

Now that the enemy has shown that they.
And in sailing so close.
In having simply sailed.

That they could even consider.
That their so-called threats.
That they might launch, and in so launching.

As such a clear need has arisen.
And in its rising.
In its staying up.

A need to negate, to nullify, to rule out.
By our having in place.
By our simply having.

Because if the enemy did.
If the enemy chose.
If, at some point, at length, the enemy.

Because whatever they might send our way.
It wouldn't take long for it to.
From the precise moment of notification.

It wouldn't be.
It would soon be.
It wouldn't.

Four minutes is all we could really expect as.
That's not sufficient for any.
In four minutes there's not enough.

In such a small window there isn't.
Hardly even to get out of. Let alone.
From that initial alarm. From our hearing.

So any counteracting measure must by needs balance out.
And our own force, already deployed, would.
Each and every, at the merest drop.

Always a few on rotation, openly.
Just circling. Waiting to.
Not wanting. But ready to.

In doing so the enemy will know.
And they can be sure that if ever they determined.
And, if so they did, then we too.

And their knowing this will ensure that.
And this in turn will dissuade them from ever.
And they must not think that we would never.

All that's needed is to hold in place.
At all hours of. At all days of.
For weeks at. For however many years.

Till the threat itself.
For so long as such a threat.
In order that such threats might be maintained.

So if indeed it came to pass.
And if it was decreed. If it was done.
Then of those procedures we have.

It would all be ready.
The decision itself would already.
And it would all be over in a flash.

In any case it just wouldn't do to be so reliant on automated
missile dumps. Each clutch of them tightly siloed, static, and
all of their noses upturned. It's far too tempting a target.

(as with matchsticks
lying snug in their box
their smooth pink heads
together seeming to yearn
for just one spark to descend
and set them all ablaze)

Keeping the bombs on the move may be easy enough.
Effective delivery is quite a separate matter. Conventional
aircraft can't sneak in that close, below radar, at speed,
without wrenching their wings. What's needed is something
to force those lower harder airs apart. Something all wing.

(as with an axe-head
its lump-iron worked
into a simple solid wedge
that digs its edge between
the wet fibres of wood
to drive them apart)

This then is left to the Vulcans. The last of the big V-bombers. The undisputed starlets of the show. Though they can't complete their act all on their own. They have their earnest accomplices, their fawning entourage.

(as with the narrowmindedness of combine harvesters
how steadily they keep their line
along the five-mile-field they've been assigned
never slowing never wavering
while little trucks and tractors
at regular intervals
rush by to tend to their needs
easing them of their grain-loads
loading up straw bales flopped out in their wake)

It's like that with the Vulcans, but reversed. First there are the Victors, old bombers themselves, now fitted for re-fuelling their sleeker sprightlier counterparts, lumbering in and out to top them up. And then there are the Argosies, repurposed from cargo to hauling comms equipment, skulking at the fringes to relay the codes.

(as with a long-distance runner
who just keeps going and going
even when down to the dregs
the fumes of reserve energy
whose team idles out at
a pre-agreed checkpoint
with flasks of essential fluid
to be clutched at and guzzled
the cartons discarded
left far behind as the runner
goes wearily endlessly galloping on)

They all have their roles. Each is in some way vital to the
work they've been given to do. Though the Vulcans take
the most acclaim. They're the ones who deliver the bombs.
They're the ones least likely to come back.

She has an easy unassuming job:
taking their dictations, filing papers,
making strong tea on request. She sets down
her tray amid a hush of deep discussion
that rises again as soon as she's pulled the door to,
ensuring they never can tell
if or when she might linger.

(. . . the draughtsman, with only
a few charcoal scratches
summons the sense of a shape)

So commonplace within their staff,
so meek, so diligent. They choose
to trust her with more sensitive documents.
Thick buff folders stamped in red,
their trailing ribbons only loosely tied.

(. . . the wine-cork presented,
an offhand sniff, a nod,
a measure poured out)

She holds the combination for the safe.
She has the knack. Can tick the dial round
with precision and haste, as effortlessly
as if she were spinning pennies on a plate.
They've been lax. They leave her
for hours alone in the office.

(. . . at the heart of the village
the beat of the blacksmith,
never missing his mark)

The warden knows her well enough
on site not to ask for her pass.
Her landlady always ensures
she eats a good breakfast,
doesn't want her fading away,
doesn't bother her when she sits
all evening cooped up in her room
pen poised over postcards:
her simplified reports, condensed
to fit within the space.

(. . . perched on the lip of the nest
the fledglings tease the air
with feathers soft and wet)

They make it too easy for her. They know
she is somebody they can rely on,
allowing her to attend the early tests,
lending her a pair of powerful binoculars,
leaving her to type up detailed observations.
Still she is cautious. Still she makes sure
she cannot be found out.

(. . . emerging from
the bitter molasses,
the brittle sugar-cube)

An open address to an aunt in the city.
Her words to be explained away
as fanciful, as mere frivolity.
No envelope for them to steam,

no microdot beneath the postage stamp.
She slips the card between the red lips
of the pillar-box in early morning,
ignoring the clink-fingered milkman
collecting the empties, who gazes,
who smiles at her as she draws near.

(. . . when no more cuts
can better its brilliance
then may the sapphire be set)

No close friends. No one her age nearby.
Only children or the very old.
And her lying long on cool summer evenings
amid the daisied grasses of the hill,
listening to the valley fill
with the rip and howl of a jet
passing by at low level.

Of the fleet there will always be five or six up. On
manoeuvres. On continuation. Very high above the Arctic.
Though not much to manoeuvre around at thirty thousand
feet. And it's far too simplistic to think of them merely
circling.

(like a column of unblinking vultures
drifting on tombstone wings
waiting for the moment to swoop in
to engage in one quick heavy dive
then to pick at whatever may be left)

Because it's never quite like that. To soar suggests slowness
and big jets don't do lazy spirals. They cut their sky-line
at eight miles a minute. The only curve they hold to is that
of the earth.

(like waterfowl like ducks
with their wide turning-circles
a constant furious flapping being
all that keeps them up or else like swans
in their hard metal whiteness
high fliers pushing on and out
from the cool dark ripply wake
of their runway lake)

From point to point, though the pilot sees nothing but sky.
The fellow behind, the maps-man with pencil and pad,
who tells the pilot where to go. The craft muscled sharply
onto a new cut at each invisible marker.

(like the workaday mallard
you never knew was there
till it bursts from its cover of reeds
tip-toeing the water to take off
to make a circuit of the trees
then softening back to the river
when nothing is found amiss)

They'll do that for hours: sketching their vapoury lines,
their giant polygons. Every while topped up by the likewise
speeding tankers. Just in case the strike-command comes
through. Keeping full-fuelled and alert in the high thin air.

And two thousand miles south
or thereabouts: a lonely Argosy
makes its own wide angular circuits,
holding well above the ocean clouds.

Not as sleek, as well-toned, as valued
as the bomber it acts as a messenger for;

, four great propellers working hard
.o drag it so fast through the air
its own ungainliness is forced aloft;
a mass not permitted to sag,
to sink back down.

And in its airy belly: ranks of bulky electronics.
Radio-transceivers. Decryption-engines. Signal-jammers.
Tele-printers with their spools of flimsy ticker-tape,
each rag-edged end poking out.

Three full sets, set apart, but with
their diodes flickering in unison.
One set as a failsafe for the next,
and the last set again for the first.

Unless, when that critical code comes through,

there is, by chance,
a fault in one of the radios
where a single valve,
unseen inside, has popped,

and elsewhere
one of the jammers
has got itself jammed,

and further down the fuselage
within the back-up of the back-up
an auto-decoder has crossed its wires
and fused a crucial component, releasing
a brief imperceptible spit of metal-smoke.

A minor break in each production-line.

So the ticker-tapes protruding stay unprinted.
Their tissued cleanliness is left to droop.

And the sudden surge of orders,
neither intercepted nor re-sent:
unnoticed, non-existent, nullified.

The aircraft sails on none-the-wiser.
No completion. Nothing to be done.

They're never all up at once, of course. Not unless attack
is imminent. Just as they're not all housed in a single spot.
Different squadrons, scattered in prime locations. As close as
can be to the target, but not too close.

(as nesting sites found near
to hunting grounds an inborn need
to be familiar with the territory
streamlines shortcuts shadows
as poachers who hug the borders
of forbidden fields who lie still
waiting watching but not too close)

A different set of codes for each squadron, based on enemy
proximity. Double-encrypted, just to be sure. A packet
of hastily gauged co-ordinates, sent via high frequency.
All speed-of-light stuff, like any radio, but better this way
for long distance.

(each set of ears attuned
tensed even when lounging
sleeping off a meal yet still
ready for that spark of noise
a prickle to pierce the calm)

Not that one can guarantee the bombers will receive it.
Not in a single frantic burst of complicated codings. Not
directly from control in any case. That's the problem with
high frequency: capricious, twitchy, painfully thin. Yes, it
might, it should, go horizontal. Or it might ping straight up
into space.

When he wakes each day he winds his watch.
The notched crown growing stubborn as
the hair-thin spring inside is coiled tight.

A precision piece, special issue for navigators,
chronographic. Its circular motions divided,
subdivided, portioned out on separate dials.

At the back of the briefing room he winds it.
The webbing unbuckled, slipped from his slender wrist.
The bright steel poised between his fingertips.

A five-loop strap in airforce grey, the scratchy nylon
softened up by sweat, by daily grime.
He cleans the casing with a cotton bud.

When there is radio-silence he winds it.
The backward ratchet tick held up to his ear outdoing
the thrum of propellers, the hurricane hiss of the air.

Its sweep-hand zeroed with a double click.
Its distance-measure matched to universal machinations
echoed by its dark insides.

When settling down for bed he winds it,
glimpsing the sharp green glow of its dials
in putting out the light.

Each minute mark, each stuttering hand,
adorned with dabs of luminescent paint.
The stored-up brightnesses of day now softly given back.

Attack plan for the Vulcans is to climb to high level
and loiter. Then if the call, the code, the command comes
through: to drop below the radar-line for final approach.
Returning once more above the clouds. If returning is
still possible.

(high and the world is made
delicate in its tinyness
an intricately moving map
an oil painting all too detailed
for its features to be resolved
its speck-shapes separated out)

In the back of the Argosy the codes-man sits with a cipher
book on one knee a puzzle book on the other. Cryptic
crosswords, complex equations, translations from Latin or
Greek. Anything to keep his mind active, heightened. Just
in case his skills are at some point required.

(low and the realities
of land and lake and hill
rush by too fast to be considered
for more than the briefest of moments
as quickly ignorable
too solid too easily broken
passed over passed through)

There's always The World Service: its reedy whine picked
up on longwave. No order not to listen. Not that such an
order could be enforced. There's comfort in the normalness
of afternoon plays, of forecasts, bulletins.

igh and the world has faded
into greyness into neutral density
its colours sun-bleached flattened out
where nothing moves and there's no longer
anywhere good to come down)

Not that a final report before the silence would help matters
much. Having heard the capital's blitzed, your hometown
gone, the fields and woods you used to walk, the families
you had no way to warn. Nothing much else to be done
beyond that. Not much point at all.

She's sitting alone in the strip-lit glare
of her kitchen when the news breaks
interrupting morning prayers.

And the warning is given,
those few minutes granted
in which there is no action left to take,
only a moment, enough, to contemplate.

So she leaves the coffee cooling,
the half-buttered toast to go soft,
and steps outside to welcome in the dawn.

(What curious hand wound up those bits
of sun and stone and sea, all packed in
tight and centrepunched, a single dot
held in a press of nothingness?)

And the doorway yields like paper, having gained
fresh insubstantiality. A silence folded, pushed aside,
admitting her into the garden, to the uncut length
of the lawn and on, beneath the sky in its uniform blue
from which the last of the starlight still shows through.

(And at that grand release when all was flung out
spinning wildly, and the planetary pieces pulled together,
and one thing led to another, who then watched them settle
into automatic motion, into perpetuity?)

Her barefoot prints bend back the grass,
the weight of one thing pressing down
to overwhelm another
and yet leaving it unharmed,

the fine green blades re-woken by
their springiness, unsticking themselves
from themselves, as from
the burdens placed upon them.

(Who rolled those planets over, examining each in turn
and with the perfect place selected then injected this
and sparked off that, promoting further change?
who moulded self-sufficiency?
who shaped the first of many replicates?)

She lingers in the moonlit shade of convenient trees.
Their purity of airs. Her slow deep breathing. Waiting
while the birds start up their noise, their dark cacophony.

(And under all heavenly spirals
and over all earthly fixations
at the tip of every motion gone before
and at the root of all directions yet to be,
did all the universe conspire to manufacture me?)

Now here the everything-she-is stands ready
for this culmination to the scheme so long ago
set on its course, for all the quicknesses in her
to be wrenched out, to leave her egg-blown.

, this shell, this dusty husk, what we've been dreaming of?)

And when the sudden sun on the horizon flashes
over hills, its wake of wind to sweep away the trees,
to open wide the doors, to silence every mouth, to whirl
right through her and keep on, she's nothing more
than grateful — that it asked so little in the end.

And somewhere reasonably distant lies the command centre.
Bunkered into borderlands in hollowed foreign soils.
Hidden by a coverlet of green to feed a scattering of cattle.
Far away from anywhere, but close enough to hear the
goings on, and always listening.

(cow bells intermittently chime
in the cloudy mountain heights
a thump of hooves comes soft
through thick stone ceilings
is mixed with the tapping of keys
a shuffle of papers under dim electric light
the stammered telegraphic beep of code)

They keep abreast of the news: the local upheavals, the
national slumps. The grit in the ointment of peaceful
protesting; the speck of mould that turns the whole batch
sour. Carnival flotillas of military might. Political gamings,
playgroundings. Of one distraction leading to another.

(the stockman is calling up the slope
he is rattling feed in a bucket
and deep under earth the sound
of ungulates lumbering downhill
comes rolling and booming
but gentled like distant explosions
like the start of the end of the world)

15

And when that balloon's puffed up too much. And when
at last it bursts. They're ready with their many monitorings.
Aware which launch-sites have been used by the arc of each
missile inbound.

(beasts clamour at the troughs
they bellow mournfully
vying for better position
a brief yet frantic moaning
before there is silence
echoing eerily downwards
sudden and prolonged)

Not that four minutes allows them the means to do much.
A cry of evacuation would be empty of any such hope. Go
where? under what? for how long? All they have left is to
order the counter attack.

Unlike earthborne vehicles of expensive pedigree
Vulcans can't stay covered up in gloom-aired garages
and only taken for a spin on sunny afternoons.

They're made to exist at maximum performance.

The heat of their flight to expand them, pushing
their patchwork plate together, a perfect seal,
becoming one seamless surface round which
the windpress passes by unhindered, unheeded.

When back on the ground they drip oil.

Each part of them cools
contracts and separates.
Natural gaps become evident.
Sharp-edged valleys in the metalwork.

ountersunk screws turn bothersome
through itchy prominence.
And so they sit in patient discomfort,
sagging their unbuoyed bulk
onto spindly wheels.

Here their dedicated ground-crews fuss.

As cleaner wrasse are permitted to scour
the skin of predatory fish,
picking parasites from gills,
dipping in and out of open jaws
to descale furred-up teeth;
likewise the men mop dribbly chins,
touch up the paintwork with artisan brushes,
buff the cockpit glass till it
is scratchless, till it mirrors emptiness.

Even a build-up of insects
mashed and hardened round the air-intakes
might alter the windflow,
might impede the perfection of flight, and so
having softened and soaped off the carapace crust
every curve is towel-dried and re-waxed.

And when with expert ear someone
detects a fine alien hum and gazing
spots the black enemy sky-speck circling
under cover of the blinding sun:

then like ants with their nest upset
who shift the exposed larvae deep under earth
so the gleams of the grounded planes,
the blank-faced bombs poised on their padded racks,
all are hastily expertly ushered indoors.

A slick operation in clearing the field
though not quite as quick as they're able:
allowing their pristine machines to be duly admired,
the bombs to be counted before they are tucked
out of sight; before the sky-speck, satisfied,
casually exits the air-space.

We have to switch radio frequencies on the hour. It avoids
unwanted detection. It's easy to do. Pre-written into charts.
Presented in a handy pocket book. Though the waves
themselves can't be hidden. Are open to anyone.

(. . . I discovered a pair of otters by the river
saw them splashing in the late evening light
their holt a hollowed trunk of hunched-up oak
I took my torch the next day got in close
found they'd delved the earth yet deeper
so many tunnels rootways hidey-holes . . .)

And out there, somewhere, are folk with ham-radio sets.
Amateurs hooking into whatever tatty threads of signal they
can find. Some only broadcast. Others are two-way.
Rambling on about anything over unseen distances. They
don't mind whom they talk to, or who listens.

(. . . can get lonely   but when we're talking   when I
your voice and   it's just a voice   I don't   I'm not
pretending we could ever   even if we   it's much too far
though sometimes I'll pretend   anywhere but here
it's fine   it's really fine and I've my responsibilities
and it's   they do depend upon me   but still I think
often   and then   back to how I   when I was alone . . .)

So, and it does happen sometimes, when switching
channels, when that hour approaches, if you turn the dial

owly, half a minute in advance, you may hit upon those
natches of chatter, fragments of far away lives.

(. . . it's become my obsession I'm out there at dawn
before work and again when I come home late
I find a spot on the bank downriver and wait
mostly see nothing just river a few dragonflies
a dipper half floating half skittering over wet stones
but I crouch very still in the long reed grass
I've nowhere else to go I can stay there for hours
till it's dark I don't mind and yet sometimes . . .)

But you never get to listen in for long. You can't risk
missing the hourly orders that may or may not be patched
through. Not on the pretext of eavesdropping, over such
ground-level utterances.

(. . . not only your voice   how you   what is it you say
I have to be cautious   makes me very   yes   a sort
a tremble   like me   when you think   it's how I   you
it could be   we could be   and I know   I feel this is
because in person   of all those other matters   maybe
we would never   we probably wouldn't have then
but even   there is this now   we are like this now . . .)

Besides which there's the need to keep an ear out for enemy
spoofing. Phoney accents slyly offering fake commands: to
give it all up: to go on home: to believe that all is well.

(. . . the setting sun was wavering and runny like egg yolk
slumping splitting sliding back and down behind the hills
its last light filtered green through a veil of beech leaves
and the river itself was a beefy brown a constant rippling
those darker patches swapping with the pale reflected blues
and I was sitting staring very still I barely even breathed . . .)

Such enemy interceptions happen infrequently. Almost not at all. Never while our team has been on shift. Though that's no reason not to expect that they might. You have to be alert to all these possibilities.

(. . . lose connection   how could I find you   if you go
how will   and where   it's troubling   then I would also
gone   unfair to say that   I know   because you might never
please don't   it's only   it should   when you're not there I'm
emptied   I've no care   it is   and all the world   and I
acting my part each day   of course   I'll do my best
to think of   in hope of   and if then someday   you . . .)

It's not about the enemy knowing when to tune in. It'd be in the avoidance of any overlap. To be hoodwinked into hearing only them. Hard to pull off, but the enemy's wily. They'll try any trick that they can, if so they can.

(. . . and realised all that riversound the sucking the splashes
the constant soft ripple even the shifting reflection itself was
an otter I was staring straight at it don't know for how long
it was playing or washing or doing whatever it is otters do
can't have known me there or if it did it didn't show it . . .)

At least the amateurs are safe enough. Safe in not talking directly to us. Speaking blind over moorland over mountain over sea. Of course they don't know that we're listening. Don't know we're here at all.

Three sets of code-breaking equipment: receiving
their ciphers simultaneously. Each one running as fast
as the next. Still their answers come out a fraction apart.
The order is different each time.

ree sets with identical problems to solve.
Whether it's a go-code or a routine. Their matched
mechanical brains spinning out ultimata. Yet here
one answer differs from the other two.

They confer. The pair in agreement strongly believe
the smallness of chance in them both being wrong
in precisely the same way proves they must be right.
They feel this logic is impeccable.

The one considers its own variation as similarly correct.
It won't be ignored. Strength of convictions combined
should not be allowed to counter that of the individual.
A truth cannot be arrived at through numbers alone.

All three agree that, in this singular instance, likelihood
must give way to perception. What was deemed improbable
is pronounced irrelevant. The possibility of any one moment
being only as real as the chosen expectations of another.

All three agree that in such a state of uncertainty
the safest solution is not to act at all, or else
to find a better way in which to run the tests,
the system having in some manner already failed.

A conclusion: reached. The go-code: not passed on.
And not a second wasted, where from without
all that's witnessed is the apparently synchronous blink
of three small amber lights, three clicks, three sudden silences.

The military state-of-mind is one of familiarity. All the daily
duties the repetitions the regular false alerts, it's all part of
desensitisation. An aircraft isn't sixty tonnes of metal kept

afloat on nothingness. It doesn't fly. Can't possibly stay up. It's merely a means of conveyance. As easy as riding a pushbike and never concerning yourself over how it maintains its relative perpendicularity. As easy as jogging without ever musing upon which muscles are needed for your legs to keep constantly moving.

(My bulk is advantageous,
when they set me going I cannot
be stopped. I must be borne
that I may then be born again,
O my creator)

Think too hard and the legs will flounder, crumple, fold, the bike will list and topple, the plane will drop out of the sky, or else, long before that, it will flop lumpily down the runway, managing no more than a few fat little leaps.

(I will not drag on updraughts.
With my nose I split the air
and sew it up behind me
seamlessly. I tidy as I go,
O my creator)

And all those bombs will be once again lifted and loaded and locked into place. Mind you they're only bombs by name, by dint of reputation. Aren't so peculiar or so cumbersome once you've hoisted them into position a hundred times over.

(I am a lozenge. I will soothe.
I am the cupboard medicine
kept in its handy packaging,
at need to be so easily pressed out,
O my creator)

ridiculous hugeness. A blunt metal smoothness. Modern sculptures, solid right the way through. That sharp knuckle-tap that sounds them out hollow is deceptive, is illusory. The hard slap that sets their skin humming is only a quirk of design, an after-effect to make them appear more vibrant, more alive.

(I am ripe. My juiciness
is packed in tight, preserved,
thick-skinned. I won't go off till I
am given to go off,
O my creator)

The military state-of-mind is one of alertness, nothing more than that. To be wound up tight one moment and then: just as tight the next. Like a dog whose ears stay pricked even while sleeping, who'll leap right out of deep dreaming and into a volley of furious barks, and all at the muffled scuttle of a mouse skipping over bare beams in the attic, or else at the wind-blown rose bush as it taps its thorny fingers on the bathroom window-pane.

(The earth is small, is soft
beneath my single heavy step.
Disorderly build-ups top the crust
but I shall blow such meagre dust away,
O my creator)

Growling and barking yet backing away from the bite. That's the aim. The undercurrent of desire. Merely to handle. Never to use. To go through all that choreography without once considering where the performance will lead; of just how long such parcels can stay lost within their delivery system; of what you become in being the dupe who jumps right to it, who steers, who pin-points, who drops.

(I am anti-bacterial.
A surface pure and bright
shall be my legacy, shall gleam
when I have made my sacrifice,
O my creator)

That's where all those dummy runs come in. A sort of
enforced thoughtlessness. So that when the order arrives
you merely do. As you've done so many times before. You
go through the moves you've perfected. Take pride in
the accuracy of your air-drawn curves. You are yourself
an instrument. Not by you: but through you. Not in you:
but of you. And then, before you know it, it's all done.

His watch gains fifteen seconds in a day.
It creeps through hours too eagerly,
a lightness to its tip-toe stepping
getting ahead of itself.

At night he matches its motions to
the pulse of an atomic clock
where forward change is marked and set
by nuclear decay,
each measure to show how far we've come
how far we've still to go.

The clock has settled its actions to that of the earth,
the earth to the universe, world to encompassing world.
Each crystal sphere to overlap yet further crystal spheres.

Through the thin glass window of his watch
he sees the distillation of those many motions,
fine white bars each moment hesitating

ɔing on again, the hidden jerk of circles
ɔurning other circles, echoed in
the repetitious instant of each individual twitch.

And as the sweep-hand hits its zero mark
he pops the crown to stop all motion dead,
listening close to the radio's tones
as he waits for the world to catch up.

In theory, pre-attack, it's done by phone. It's political.
They're aware of any threat. They know of its seriousness.
They're monitoring. They're marking off the stages as they
pass. They're tied into negotiations, trying to calm matters
by talk, by diplomatic argy-bargy, by offers, by reasonable
compromise. But always with the military hovering,
looming, listening in.

(as with a mess of cotton thread
extracted from a sewing bag
despite the interweaving loops
the coils the undue complications
at first it all seems manageable
each knot has a visible structure
a line leading in and a line leading out)

In theory, when the enemy doesn't back down, when into
one telephone they say one thing and into another they're
all set to relay the order to launch, even though they won't
want to show their true intent, our lot have to read that
intent, true or otherwise, our lot have to be ready to react
the very same second, and the enemy needs to know that
they'll react, that they're ready, that the intent is being
heard, that what's implied matches with what's inferred.

(and at a point in the unravelling where it's clear
the lines have tangled themselves beyond reason
there's still a hope that some of these new knots
are not knots at all that they're deceptions and
that pulling them all yet tighter will show
how suddenly with a soft snap each slips free
how one sharp tug will make them disappear)

In theory the command centre needs to be given the code
by which they may access the codes in order to patch them,
coded, to the already airborne Argosies, where they will
be decoded, verified, confirmed, re-coded, and sent on to
the bombers. And all this will be happening, all will be set
in place, playing out. At least to a point. Each stage
completed up to that final stage, the one from which it's
impossible to climb down.

(even when at length the string has set
into its undoable mess the knots so small
and tight they seem like junctions as if
the strands have fused together even then
there's still that clear thread running out
the part untroubled untouched to be followed
while the rest is cut off and discarded)

In theory once the Vulcans have their orders they're off.
No turning away and no recall. They make themselves deaf
to further commands. They have their line to follow.
And they do. Their dip, their sudden lift, their drop, their
looping back again.

She is just stepping into the bath
when the lights go out.
The dark that's left behind
profoundly fixed.

nd with that last long certainty
pronounced, inbound, and counting down,
can I be sure that really
there is nothing to be lost?)

She slides herself into the nowhere
of water made thick with magnesium salts.
The deformed remnants of a bath-bomb
fizzing by her feet.

(What was the state of play before
the advent of the zero-hour?
What was the accident
that spilled existence into being?)

Settling, stretching her limbs into unfeeling space.
Her buoyancy, her body-heats, both matched.

(What need for anything but stone?
what need to cover stone with slime?
what need for slime to learn to swim?
to stand? what need to speak?)

She can't feel the bath-tub, can't even be certain
of the room the bath-tub sits within.
The sides, the ceiling,
the sense of herself — all gone.

(If I'm no more than just another crumb
of wayward space-coagulum
what makes my fleshiness more special
than some other higher state of energy?)

The water keeps soundlessly rising, expanding
and carrying her along with it.

(What creatures might emerge
from resolutions we've agreed? is our
intelligence a blip in the momentousness
of matter and its fitful composites?)

The poundings of her heart grow soft.
Her thoughts thin through the spreading warmth.
Her muddled physicalities, now eased
into a single deep dark pool.

(Won't we be glad at last to see the light?
Will gladness prove to be more than
an impulse? Is there glue enough
to hold us to this path?)

The lights stay off, the calm new-split
by water-suck, by splashes, as
she reaches out a hand and blindly
drops another bomb into the bath.

Their radar, our radar, prime targets, both. If the sweep of
their sightlines can be taken out with your first prudent
release, your one-time cursory lob, then what comes after
is a free-for-all.

(thirty black specks from the outside
drawing in skimming over the enemy turf
with their speck-shadows dipping and rising
a hesitant shivery retinue small black flies
never flagging always managing to keep up)

The radio's more than a messaging service. It acts as the end
of an ever extendable rope on which one may tug,
reassuringly. Then at least if bomber-command are still
talking: we know that the world is still working.

rty black specks all converging little
usters moving over the map of the land
each one extinguished with a small white flash
their inverse inkblots spreading out and merging
till every square of the earth has been bleached)

At each appointed change of frequencies: a pause before
connection is confirmed. A few heavy seconds of space-
filling static. A purr. And then a voice.

Above the cloud level
a broad-shouldered Victor.
Its fuel-line stiffly extended
trailing in the hard backdraught.
An untrimmed umbilicus.
A heron's dangled legs.
Beyond its open end a Vulcan
closing the gap by inches.
The cup for the fuel-line wavering near
to the tip of the Vulcan's nose.
On the edge of the stratosphere
an enemy spy-plane.
Its underside freckled
with several small peep-holes.
Enemy agents lying on cushions
watch through telescopic lenses.
They scribble into notepads.
They focus on the ever-narrowing gap
between nozzle and cup.
A slow-motion creep.
Cloud-wisps whip back round the Vulcan
to the high whine of concordant engines.
Wind-rush splitting over intakes.
Far off the spy-plane is silent.
It observes silently.

A distant spectacle played through
without accompaniment.
The end of the fuel-line quivers, settles.
The stout probe on the nose of the Vulcan
sniffs at the connection point,
moves a little closer,
kisses the rim of the aperture.
Metal touching metal.
The spies demist their eye-pieces.
They look again.
They zoom in.
The Vulcan pushes forward.
The cup for the fuel-line
presenting itself, allowing
the acorn-ended nozzle
to ease still deeper in.
The two large aircraft coupling with
a small soft suck. An unheard click.
The spies scribble fervidly.
The scratch of pen-nibs mixed up
with the sound of heavy breathing.
The Victor and the Vulcan tied
by a single thin black line.
Unseen fluids are pumped
from one to the other.
The two machines submitting
to a matched velocity.
The spies hold their breath.
They hold gold watches, round
and heavy, veined ornately,
twitching in their palms, marked off
when fresh air is glimpsed
at the far end of the fuel-line.
As the Vulcan timidly withdraws.
As the hose is retracted,

and again thickly
to the Victor's belly.
And the spies close their notepads.
They sit back, they sigh,
avoiding eye-contact.
The viewing-holes covered over.
Drinks poured tentatively out.
A record slid with care
onto a spindle.
A needle lowered
into a fine spiral groove.

The bomb itself is no fancy rocket. Can't be simply pointed and let loose. It will not follow a scent of its own accord. It is sightless and flightless and witless and fat. Must have its hand held all the way and only let go for those few final seconds. The one sure thing it knows how to do is fall.

(the last land-hugging stretch
near supersonic through the thicker airs
sweeping a wake over forest-tops
like fingers trailed through water
rattling the church-spire's copper cross
spinning the farm's weathervane
a pregnant approach
the speed of the carrier
being the speed of the bomb
floated soft and belly-held and effortless)

And when those bombs are trolleyed out. When with pride they're presented, polished, lined up, ready for loading. When each seems spotless, each externally identical. Then which to select? Which should be inserted dumbly into the hollow embrace of each aircraft's warm and welcoming insides?

(a sudden stiff climb the start
of a perfectly drawn parabola where
at the steepest point the bomb is released
an easy underarm toss a graceful
weightlessness as it completes the upper arc
of the curve on which it's been set
as its envoy rolls off the top of the throw
and peels away homewards standing by
for the blast-wave to give it a boost)

There's only chance enough for a single deployment. They
carry no spare. They've no alternative. The first shall be
the last. A neat no-nonsense detonation: that is all that's
required. Not to be fumbled and dropped premature in the
ocean. Not to let that overbearing bulk clog up the hatch.
Not to fizzle out on impact, leaving no more than a dent.

He has opened his watch beneath the narrow cone
of yellow light from a lamp tilted low to the table.

He has unscrewed the back-plate, relieving the slippery
black rubber o-ring squashed against the finely threaded rim.

He has laid bare all the inner convolutions.
Their unseen secrets tarnished by his look.

Overlapping interlocking wafers of metallic viscera.
A wishbone heart, see-sawing its forward intent.

Fixed amid these jagged palpitations, a delicate
ruby-mounted lever. Adjusted for loss or for gain.

Nudge it one way: the watch's world spins faster.
Nudge it the other: it flags.

toothpick, lowered through this sensitive interior.
ϫs dull wooden tip soft-pressed to the tip of the lever.

So small an adjustment he does not see it move.
Nor does he feel it. Nor can he be certain if it has.

A shift the width of an atom. No more than a touch.
The merest suggestion of motion. A willing. A want.

The toothpick withdrawn, the rear plate screwed on,
he waits for change through slow agglomeration.

How swiftly the world may now run on without him.
To what degree he is able to hold himself back.

Of course the enemy always makes its move at night.
They're crafty like that. It may not be the decent thing
but it does at least make sense. Ramping up the tensions
while we're sleeping. Putting our officials into a dither.
So that the phones are all buzzing. The whole air ringing.
Lines and crossed-lines. Everything in a tangle, already taut,
yet getting still gradually tighter.

(out of the dark the call comes
wailing sirens pushing through and into
semi-wakefulness all dream-hazed
each man tumbled out of bed
straight into flight-suits heavy boots
sleep-running in the blue-lit spin
of night's unbounded void then bundled
up into the stuffy fuel-aired paunch
of the waiting machines their thin skins
trembled by the slow-grown warmth
of ground-power's ready hum)

A two-hour notification. So it's pretty serious. Emergent, yes, though not yet imminent. And no one any closer to knowing just how it may turn out. Those already up and circling are in the same stretched state of ignorance as those still stuck on the tarmac. Sharpening their ears to any radio crackle that might somehow resolve itself into an order, a go-command, or else, after hours of rigid inconclusive watchfulness, for the eventual call to climb down.

(a steady loosening of stand-by strings
the crowded blacks of night give way
to growing light blue-grey blue-white
the nervous buzz of power
cut replaced on exit by the noise
of many birds their piercing lines
crisscrossing in the new-stirred air
the dark green tracks scuffed into grass
each path retraced each mattress sag
each hot-socked boot slipped off)

Whether false alarm or exercise or diplomatic ruse, it all turns out the same. For those on shift to do the work they're kept in place to do. Every call's a real call. Every action: reaction. All they've been accustomed to withhold. How with just a word they might release it. And at the point of sleep: that same uncomfortable reflection on whatever the night may bring. Of what may flare up with the dawn. A prickle, a flush, a fine heat beneath the skin. Sensed just at the moment of drifting off.

She hears of the warning one moment before
she burrows into bed. As such
she chooses not to heed it. Folding instead
the quilt yet tighter in around her.
Making a cool nest of pillows for her cheek.

light of inescapable destruction
hat use is contemplating anything
when all I may consider will be swept out
as effectively
as all that goes ignored?)

One eye open, peeking from a twitch of sheets,
she sees in the sodium glow those night-shapes
made out of the pieces of her room. Less detailed
than their daytime counterparts, but real enough:
her apprehensiveness, her dread made manifest.

(If all I know exists within myself,
if everything external can be reappraised
as any simple wonder
I might draw inside a dream,
then isn't it about time I woke up?)

A muffle of argument from the rooms below.
Not argument but rushed cooperation.
Not cooperation but confusion. A panic, brief
then suddenly halted. Now a flustering of feet.
Now the unceremonious soft slam of a door.

(If what I am is made of memory,
my stacked experiences, personal or pinched,
and if I'll never get to pass each grain of data on,
and since I won't be there to know them gone,
what should I care that I'll be going too?)

And all her guarded murmurations
echo undiminished in her heart's deep cavities.
And of a neckline's dark indent. And of the scents
and softnesses once stolen from the dip and roll
of a shoulder. Every captured aspect, similarly stored.

(To wait, to watch, to move, it makes no odds.
Each state no more occurrent than the next.
Unless to be here is about the same
as being there. Can being nowhere
really make a difference in the end?)

Dampened by the wall beside her bed
the sound of sobbing, like the whining
of a wounded animal, broken by soft hiccups of despair.
It pauses in uncertainty. It tests the new silence
with sniffles. It goes on again.

(And what if I admitted giving up?
how long ago I'd ceased all worrying
of what I will or what I won't become.
And in the utter calm that followed — I
had found a way to cope, to carry on.)

A fine rain beaten sideways by the wind
sticks its beading to her window with the gentle sound
of rice poured hesitatingly into a pan.
Each freshly stippled pane of glass
disrupting the light coming in.

(And if I wished myself beneath the earth,
if that proved safer in the end;
if I was separated out and scattered, living then
as dust, in hope someone might breathe me in;
who'd choose to gather every little piece?)

The purpose is reactive: to hold in place: to deter. But even
when in place, if deterrence alone proves ineffectual (and
matters may indeed sometimes get fraught), if the
information concerning the enemy's intention is persuasive,

e evidence overwhelming, then it's also possible to jump
he gun, to get in first. To win the war before there is a war.

(There's no incentive to go looking for a reason.
Though such action may at least be reasonable.
And good reason shouldn't have to be excused.)

And once it's done it's done. If the call goes out it can't be
re-called. That's one of the basic rules. Can't have the
bombers yo-yoing. Can't be forever crying wolf. It'd make
a mockery of the whole operation. So, if they go: they go.

(And if that's what the intelligence shows.
If it shows categorically. Indisputably.
Then we must trust to our intelligence.)

And if the order proves to be a mistake (because mistakes
can, will, and do happen), if the enemy changes its mind
(because even the enemy is capable of recognising its own
foolhardiness), the decent thing might be to let them know
what's heading their way. Or else perhaps to hold our
tongue. They'll find out soon enough. Or not at all. No
need to fuel more nonessential angst.

(The threat, as such, will have been eliminated.
Because the threat, if anything, was always real.
And threats, in all seriousness, can't go ignored.)

The question of blame in such matters has several strands.
Who shoved whom the hardest? Whose strategy was bound
up with pretence? Who thought it sensible to have such
weapons openly in stock? Who loved their country the
most? Who loved life more? It makes no difference how it's
asked, the answers get us nowhere in the end.

His watch as near to true as he can set it
by which he gets a fix upon the stars,
ensuring they are where they ought to be.

Keeping the lamplight dim so his eyes stay bright.
Enough to read the pad upon his knee,
his pencilled sums, his pre-drawn charts.

The pattern of glowed green dots on the watchface,
the narrow field of stars seen in
the six-inch circle of the periscope.

Each star in a ceaseless self-contained explosion,
a reliable spot in the universal spin,
as pin-heads hammered flush into the black.

Each an anchor point, a hole
through which light bleeds
and escapes.

Holes into which may be hooked
fine threads of quintessence,
the intricate lines overlapping to form

an ever-divergent mesh.
A spacious weave on which to sail.
Easy to break. Easy to sew back up.

Caught deep within a corner of this net:
a routine night-flight, idling,
tracing its roundabout course.

His angular reading of the stars
matched to the mechanics of his watch.
Their subtle movement worn upon his wrist.

nd all this just to find out where they are
and where they're going to
and how long it will take.

When things start getting thick on the phones then all
the bombers in each squadron take off together. At once.
En masse. Seven hulking Vulcans. All sitting in a line. Like
a curiously-sectioned caterpillar. Each free-floating segment
hoping the next one along won't suddenly falter.

(a weak-limbed crumple
a seizure a stubborn resolve
and they shunt they buckle
they nestle together
stacking like paper cups)

Because they all have to start moving simultaneously. One
body. One long slick machine. Every well-tended engine
at maximum thrust. A line of fat white triangles stencilled
neatly onto the runway. First sliding, then lifting, then
peeling away from the world.

(and their sensitive cargoes
picked free from the wreckage
are hug-hurried over the grass
to be stashed out of sight
squirrelled off for safe keeping)

Because it's hard to steer a Vulcan when it's hurtling down
the concrete. It needs to be up. So, before they've tucked
a good bit of air beneath their wings, while they're still
earthbound and heavy, if the one at the head of the queue
promptly splutters and fails, with all the others coming up
fast behind it: then that's the game finished. A foot-fault
embarrassment. All points passed on to the opposing side.

39

Some folk only join up for the flying.
The basic training, the officer classes, the trials, the tests:
it's endured, it's enjoyed.
In the knowledge of where it will lead.
As a means to an end.

Really, for them, it's only the flying that matters,
they're not so keen when it comes to the sharp-end stuff.
Not quite non-combatants. Not even objectors.
They accept the principle of their role
despite a deep-seated discomfort.

But when a code comes chattering through,
its fine grey type imprinted
onto a thin white papery strip;
and when this time it's the right code, the go-code,
no war-game scenario, no mere exercise:

there should be no hesitation,
no alternative to consider;
the reaction needs to be immediate,
the destruction: absolute.

Still, the pilot does consider, because
to be a pilot is to make many quick considerations
from moment to moment, and no less for this.

So as swiftly as the order tickers through
the pilot chooses to ignore it.

But there are measures set in place for this sort of thing.
One never acts alone: command
may shift, or else coercion
may be employed by dint
of a warm pistol muzzle

essed to the back of the head, except
who'd really concede to do that?

And if, by chance, in that instant, the co-pilot
arrives at the same no-go decision;
and if then the wiresman, the aimer, the plotter,
if each is found to be, individually,
in perfect agreement:
then very soon the interstice of action will have passed.

Five singular minds coinciding. A natural accord.
Not a matter of bare disobedience, one clear choice:
not to do what they've been tasked to do.

Perhaps they could argue the code itself
never came through.
Perhaps they might somehow produce
an alternative slip of ticker-tape
to prove they thought the order had been false.

A predilection for returning to face
due discipline, rather than playing their part;
or for whatever else may remain
when at length they do get back.

The worst sort of weather is that which can't be predicted.
Can't be seen. Doesn't really exist. Till you're already right
in amongst it. Example: icing-up at altitude. Above the high
cloud line. A column of sky at saturation point might stay
that way if not for the cool-skinned Argosy blundering into
an otherwise empty blueness.

(there are sundogs on the horizon
our star split into three and each one
standing guard beyond the atmosphere)

Like a furred-up freezer chest, only inside out. The wet air finds its surface: sticking itself to the sub-zero metal. Adhering in plaques, in crystal laminates. Slicks of ice, new-forming, over ice. So the finer joints start to seize: ailerons, elevators, trim-tabs, etc. All of them soon rendered useless.

(a rainbow having broken its moorings
to pull away clear from the earth now floats free
and full as the ring it always strained to be)

Not that the loss of roll-capability matters quite so much. The main problem is the sheer weight of it. That and the altered aerodynamics. The bulked-up leading edges of wings and propellers. The four dart engines struggling to shake this new coverall from their calibrated blades.

(the full moon has a misty corona
soft concentric circles blueing outward
from a faultless bright white core)

So, like the lumpwork of metal it basically is, the aircraft starts to fall again, back down to earth. As though it had only just realised its own airborne impossibility. A slow three-mile drop. Except on plunging through the warmer airs the ice begins creaking and snapping and slipping away.

(a few more degrees and the sundogs flare and vanish
the rainbow inverts to spill its inner colours into space
the moon is blotted out by thick black cloud)

A brittle skin being shed in huge white slabs. And when the ice spins off the propellers it splinters and smacks right into the fuselage. Like a heavy rain of machine-gun fire. The racket inside so fierce you'd think the war had already begun.

1 air-show, sunkissed and sticky, its hot concrete
ordered with gaudy spectators.

The family-man with a girl on his shoulders.
The obsessive with tripod and super-8 camera.

Businessfolk on complimentary tickets, who sip
in the parasolled shade of picketed enclosures.

A woman half-in/half-out of her grass-parked car,
iced bun in one hand, field-glasses firm in the other.

And the team of red gnats have shown off their tight
and all-too-familiar formations.

And there have been daredevils, and deafenings,
and blubbing children placated with ice-cream.

And somewhere about sits a long white prototype,
although it isn't scheduled to go up.

Then comes the one they're all really here for.
Even for those who know nothing about it:

they soon have that sense of uncanny importance
if not from the crowding and craning then from

its overbearing presence
and the whisper of its name.

A curious giant that looks like a fighter
and flies like a fighter: all single-stick stuff,

all muscle and self-centred poise; the way
it strokes the sky with dreamy composure;

the way its crew-bubble, squashed up into its snout,
seems more like an offhand inclusion, an afterthought.

And yet for all these endowments
not a fighter. Far too big for a start.

The audience willing it into performance,
wanting to hear it, to feel it, the roaring, the howl

that sounds more like a moan. A mournful cry
from the stresses of its envelope-pushing display.

Like a pony made to turn tight circles
not by gentle persuasion but by

the sharpness of the bit that tugs
and cuts into the corners of its mouth.

A tired old beast forced into the tricks of its youth.
The tricks it was never designed for

but still it could do them, does do them.
Spectacular even in semi-retirement.

The visible weight of it. A ponderous slowness
that somehow looks graceful, that looks

like it hangs in the air, when really
it's straining through every moment to stay up.

A pure excess of power that pressures it
into its final stunt, a near-vertical climb, and how

at the cloud-nudging apex it seems to lose power:
a swoon, a dead faint, slipping back

...id then rolling off sharply, its nose pointed earthwards
...t full thrust, to pull itself

heavily into the clear,
to the unheard applause of the crowd, very small

far below, who seek only now to acknowledge
the peril that has been averted.

When it comes down to it so many things can go wrong.
Chaotic it may be, but preferable to automation, to the
effortless flick of a switch. Much better to rely on the inborn
reluctance of each and every man. And there aren't any
orders as such, not for how one behaves. Somewhere,
by that point, it's already over. A country gone quiet.
A dimple. A smouldering plain.

(an island picked out
small and mountainous
near enough to nowhere
ignorable forgettable
a hesitant descent
through high valley mists
and onto a short black runway
no guide-lines no lamps
no sign of anyone)

There's not really any survival gear to speak of, not on
board. No flimsy A-frame tent. No cooking pots. Not even
basic rations. Little point in loading up supplies when a
full-blown attack won't leave much to live for. If you're
lucky you may find a few bars of chocolate, hidden away
in a tin. But that's been there for a good few years. By now
it likely tastes of kerosene. Everything seems to get tainted
after a while.

(women in national dress
green-eyed freckled pig-tailed
presenting local wares
to the stiff-limbed crew
a fish-supper shared
down by the harbour wall
as they gaze out over
the black lapping waves
towards phosphorescent horizons)

You'll hear it in those last communications. Not the
wording itself but the tone that tells you it's true. A forced
rigidity applied to over-rehearsed commands. Fully aware
that they'll be a primary target. Their location well known
to the enemy, who'll still hope to limit the extent of
retaliation, even though they know what's coming next.

Yet here, for her, it is a night
on which there is no warning given,
and the silence is no different
from all other nightly silences.

The routine of her day completed
as it thickens round her into routine loneliness.
Except, on this one night, she's not alone.

(All effort is of little worth
if only meant to satisfy the self.
My own internalised contentment
only comes from how the outside
may impress upon it.)

And now it's she who switches out the light
and locks the door and draws the heavy curtains
very nearly closed.

Each action ordered to her deft creation
of a space in which
no one exists but them.

Their nearness necessary
in the dimming of a world new-made,
each wondering what it is the other sees,
each breathing in the air the other breathes.

(And could the sudden stealing of a kiss
be meant as nothing more
than one's desire for drawing breath
directly from the source?)

To ask to hold in hope to touch
a heartbeat other than one's own.

When breathing inward presses out
it's only fair to wish
once started
such proximity might never end.

(And if it fell to nothing, if the air
turned stale, the grasses then
so many miles of dust, and if I walked
would there be hope in finding anyone at all?
would it be foolish just to try?)

How still they stand,
one's fingers pushing backward
slowly through the other's hair.
And of such stillness, of such touch,
it's here they find
there is no need, no want,
for any more than this.

(Even in a wilderness I'd feel that spark
that sense of someone else still being there.
With all that's bound between us
would it be so strange to wonder if
we'd speak or see each other once again?)

A face dipped forward to a face reclined.

Her lifted eyes, both cool and wide
to counteract the dark.
                              And if no words
are in and of that closeness spoken
then there's no way to be certain
that their thoughts are likewise matched.

(How close things draw together just to split.
How full an understanding of the ways in which
our worlds may pull apart.
If everything we strove for led to this
how could it be undone with one embrace?)

The curtains yield a narrow gap
through which the thin white street-lamp light
illuminates the pair, enough
to know each other there —

what then is lost by letting all that light flood in.